My State OREGON

By Christina Earley

TABLE OF CONTENTS

A Crabtree Seedlings Book

Crabtree Publishing
crabtreebooks.com

School-to-Home Support for Caregivers and Teachers

This book helps children grow by letting them practice reading. Here are a few guiding questions to help the reader build his or her comprehension skills. Possible answers appear in red.

Before Reading:

• What do I know about Oregon?
  • *I know that Oregon is a state.*
  • *I know that Oregon has mountains.*

• What do I want to learn about Oregon?
  • *I want to learn which famous people were born in Oregon.*
  • *I want to learn what the state flag looks like.*

During Reading:

• What have I learned so far?
  • *I have learned that Salem is the state capital of Oregon.*
  • *I have learned that Crater Lake formed from a volcanic eruption.*

• I wonder why...
  • *I wonder why the state flower is the Oregon grape.*
  • *I wonder why Thor's Well makes the ocean look like it disappears.*

After Reading:

• What did I learn about Oregon?
  • *I have learned that Oregon grows the most Christmas trees in the U.S.*
  • *I have learned that the state animal is the beaver.*

• Read the book again and look for the glossary words.
  • *I see the word **capital** on page 6, and the word **eruption** on page 15. The other glossary words are found on pages 22 and 23.*

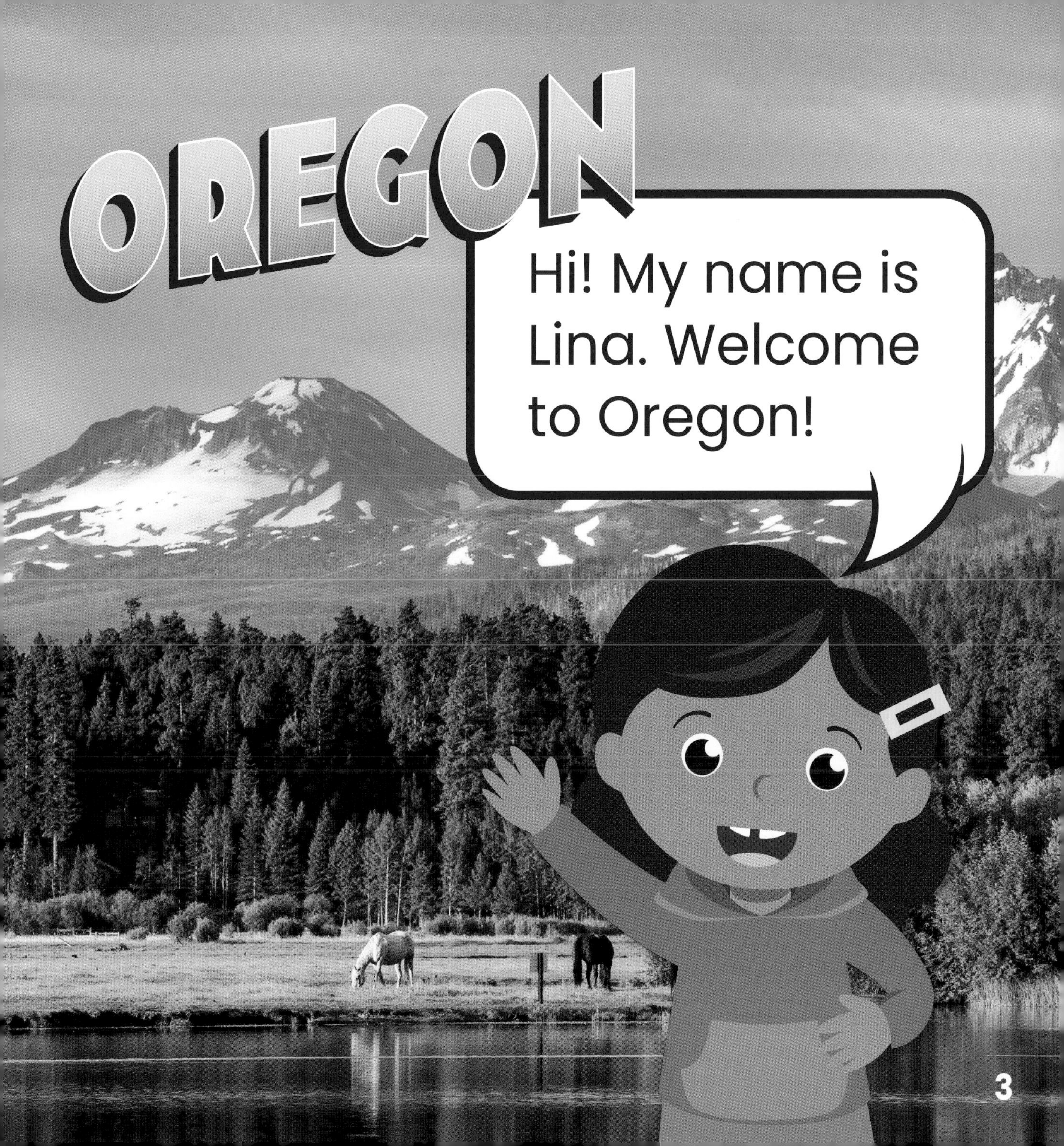
OREGON
Hi! My name is Lina. Welcome to Oregon!

I live in Bend. My city is on the Deschutes River.

I can see a **volcano** called Tumalo Mountain from my house.

Salem

Oregon is in the northwestern United States. The **capital** is Salem.

Fun Fact: Portland is the largest city in Oregon.

The state animal is the beaver.

The Oregon grape is the state flower.

We grow a lot of Christmas trees in Oregon. Oregon grows the most Christmas trees in the United States.

Fun Fact: About 5 million Christmas trees are grown in Oregon each year.

My state flag is blue. Part of the state **seal** is on the front and a beaver is on the back.

My family enjoys watching the Portland Trail Blazers play basketball.

I like to visit Crater Lake National Park. I enjoy hiking the trails.

Fun Fact: Crater Lake formed from a volcanic **eruption**.

A **sinkhole** at Thor's Well makes the ocean look like it disappears.

Haystack Rock has **tide pools** to explore.

Phil Knight, the co-founder of Nike, was born in Oregon. Author Beverly Cleary was also born in Oregon.

Fun Fact: Mary Jane Spurlin, who became Oregon's first woman judge in 1926, was born in Salem, Oregon.

Snowboarding on Mt. Bachelor is exciting!

I enjoy watching the sea lions at Sea Lion Caves.

capital (cap-ih-tuhl): The city or town where the government of a country, state, or province is located

eruption (ih-ruhp-shun): A sudden explosion of rocks, ash, and lava from a volcano

seal (seel): A special design that is used on important papers and other items

sinkhole (singk-hohl): A hole in the ground that is formed when dirt and rocks are washed away by flowing water

tide pool (tied pool): A shallow pool of seawater

volcano (vol-kay-noh): A mountain with an opening that sometimes sends out an explosion of lava, rocks, and ash

Index

About the Author

Christina Earley lives in sunny South Florida with her husband and son. She enjoys traveling around the United States and learning about different historical places. Her hobbies include hiking, yoga, and baking.

Written by: Christina Earley

Designed and Illustrated by: Bobbie Houser

Series Development: James Earley

Proofreader: Melissa Boyce

Educational Consultant: Marie Lemke M.Ed.

Photographs:
Alamy: Everett Collection Inc: p. 18 left; Historic Collection: p. 18 right; Archive PL: p. 19
Newscom: Brian Rothmuller/Icon Sportswire DHZ: p. 13
Shutterstock: Marisa Estivill: cover; Bob Pool: p. 3; Cascade Drone Photography: p. 4-5, 23; Volina: p. 6, 22; Sean Pavone: p. 7; Christian Musat: p. 8; Randy Bjorklund: p. 9; Jamie Hooper: p. 10-11; Bandersnatch: p. 11; railway fx: p. 12, 22; Zhukova Valentyna: p. 14-15; Wollertz: p. 15, 22; lu_sea: p. 16, 23; Anton Rogozin: p. 17, 23; Sveta Imnadze: p. 20; B Norris: p. 21

Crabtree Publishing

crabtreebooks.com   800-387-7650

Copyright © 2024 Crabtree Publishing

Printed in the U.S.A./072023/CG20230214

Published in Canada
Crabtree Publishing
616 Welland Avenue
St. Catharines, Ontario
L2M 5V6

Published in the United States
Crabtree Publishing
347 Fifth Avenue
Suite 1402-145
New York, New York, 10016

Library and Archives Canada Cataloguing in Publication
Available at Library and Archives Canada

Library of Congress Cataloging-in-Publication Data
Available at the Library of Congress

Hardcover: 978-1-0398-0531-6
Paperback: 978-1-0398-0563-7
Ebook (pdf): 978-1-0398-0627-6
Epub: 978-1-0398-0595-8